RUNAWAYS

WRITER **BRIAN K. VAUGHAN**
PENCILS **ADRIAN ALPHONA**
INKER **CRAIG YEUNG**

COLORIST CHRISTINA STRAIN LETTERER VIRTUAL CALLIGRAPHY'S RANDY GENTILE
COVER ARTIST JO CHEN

EDITORS MACKENZIE CADENHEAD & C.B. CEBULSKI

RUNAWAYS CREATED BY BRIAN K. VAUGHAN & ADRIAN ALPHONA

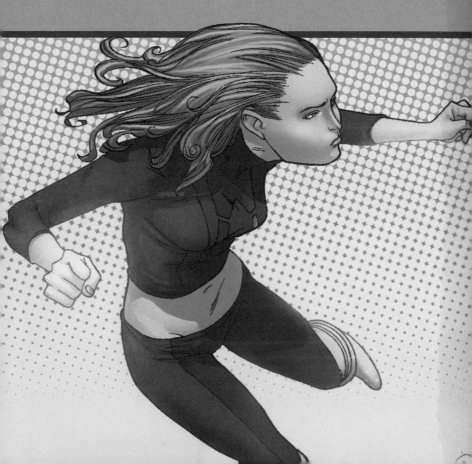

Collection Editor: Jennifer Grünwald
Editorial Assistants: James Emmett & Joe Hochstein
Assistant Editors: Alex Starbuck & Nelson Ribeiro
Editor, Special Projects: Mark D. Beazley
Senior Editor, Special Projects: Jeff Youngquist
Vice President of Sales: David Gabriel
SVP of Brand Planning & Communications: Michael Pasciullo
Book Design: Jeff Powell

Editor in Chief: Axel Alonso
Chief Creative Officer: Joe Quesada
Publisher: Dan Buckley
Executive Producer: Alan Fine

Us?

Ma'am, how are *we* supposed to stop something if the *grown-up* us's can't?

You have to find Victorious when *he* was just a boy... before he becomes too strong...

His real name is *Victor Mancha.*

He grew up... here in Los Angeles...

Don't trust him. He's not who he says he is... I knew only *you guys* would understand...

His father... is a *villain* from your time... the greatest *evil*... in the *universe*...

What's that *mean?* Who's this guy the son of?

Sweet Chase...

In all those years... I never told you... how much I loved...◇

2

I haven't been able to find any footage of Chase Stein, the girls' getaway man... but seeing how he's the son of two mad scientists, we're guessing that he's the *brains* of the operation.

According to records I dug up through work, Chase and his friends are all children of *The Pride*, the underworld syndicate most of us learned about for the first time on the news last summer.

Details are sketchy, but after running away from these villains, the kids apparently *destroyed* their parents. Since then, they've disappeared from their foster homes, eventually resurfacing with Los Angeles' most recent *crime wave*.

God, I can't imagine how Power Pack would have turned out if *my* folks had been evil.

I don't know, Julie. Maybe that's why these guys are fighting crime now... to make up for the bad stuff their moms and dads did, you know?

Or maybe they're just eliminating the *competition* so they can pick up where The Pride left off.

Unfortunately, that's a possibility, Chris.

But either way, an anonymous donor promised to give *one million dollars* if we get these kids safely off the streets.

I didn't believe it, but this guy's already sent Mickey a $10,000 cashier's check as an advance.

So now we're bloody *bounty hunters*? I thought this little club of former capes-and-tighters was supposed to be *pro bono*.

I don't miss Gen X, but at least we never heroed for *dollars*.

Starsmore's got a point, Phil. Besides, how do we know the dude we're taking cash from isn't, like, some old *friend* of The Pride, looking to get payback on their kids?

Because he didn't ask us to *murder* them, Johnny. By all accounts, this is just a *Good Samaritan* who wants to help kids like us get into healthy, stable environments.

And we're *not* doing it for personal gain. Whatever money we make will go towards opening up *more* branches of our organization.

We could be a national network helping recovering teen heroes all across the country...

...not a third-rate support group that has to meet in my cousin's *garage*.

3

4

You don't know what you're talking about, little girl!

That's a *Rick Jones* song!

Superfreak?

That's *Rick James.* Geez, haven't any of you guys read *Sidekick?*

Rick Jones has only lived, like, the *dream* existence. He was part of the Avengers when he was *our* age. He got to hang with Thor, Iron Man... he was Captain America's *partner!*

SIDE KICK

RICK JONES

We met Captain America once. He made us go into *foster care* after our parents got blown up trying to destroy the world.

He had really bad breath.

Victor, if you have such a man-crush on the Spandex crowd, why do you want to *murder* all of them when you grow up?

Why do you people keep saying that?

I'm *not* a criminal. I've never even had *detention* before! I mean, everybody in my class thinks I'm a *narc.* I--

Tray tables stowed and seatbacks up, ladies!

My dad was a U.S. Marine who *died* in the Panama Invasion when I was just a baby.

You have any *evidence* to back that up?

You have any evidence to prove I'm *wrong?*

How about Gert totally coming back from the future Terminator-style? She said your old man was the greatest evil in the universe.

I told you, my mom is an architect's assistant by day, a student by night, and a waitress by *later* at night.

And I reserve the word "evil" for very few things outside of fat-free ice cream and non-Mac computers.

I know it's tough to swallow, Victor, but *trust us,* you can live a whole lifetime with your parents and still not know the first thing about them.

And if you never even got the chance to *meet* one of 'em...

Nico, can't you just cast a magic—something to *show* us his past?

Sorry, Mol, I already used my one shot with that spell on Future Gert.

If we're gonna uncover the truth, we'll have to do the one thing I never thought we'd do again.

Homework.

Well, that's a possibility, but let's stick to the ne'er-do-wells for now.

...as soon as I figure out how to advance to my next selection on this stupid thing.

Huh. Well, if you're a gadget geek, maybe you're the son of *this* whack-job, a gamma-irradiated egghead imaginatively named *The Leader.*

Here, fork it over. That's a black-market universal remote from *Wakanda.* I read the specs online last year. Their *OS* is a little tricky.

Nah, Mancha's got *brawn* to go with his brains... not to mention whatever x-factor let him wallop Karolina with those metal bleachers.

Maybe he's the son of *Norman Osborn.* You know, that corporate bruiser who used to dress up in a bad Halloween costume?

Why are we only considering men from *this* planet? I thought you said Vic's father was the biggest bad in the *universe.*

Good point, K. Pull up File 31, would you, Victor?

I used to think this was just an urban legend, but our parents wrote that one of the greatest threats ever to come to Earth was *this* thing...

HARDCOVER VOL. 2 COVER SKETCH BY ADRIAN ALPHONA

HARDCOVER VOL. 2 COVER BY ADRIAN ALPHONA & CHRISTINA STRAIN

"TRUE BELIEVERS, CHAPTER ONE"

THE FULL SCRIPT FOR (NEW) RUNAWAYS #1
PREPARED FOR MARVEL COMICS
SEPTEMBER 21, 2004

[Welcome back, everybody! Adrian, this first script is a big one, but it's got a lot of fun $#%@ in it, and mostly pages made up of four panels or less, so hopefully, you can burn right through it. We've got a lot of new characters to introduce, but that's what you're best at, so I know you'll knock this one out of the park. Have fun!]

PAGE ONE

Page One, Panel One

      Okay, we open with this page-wide, letterbox, establishing shot of Downtown Los Angeles, maybe a smaller version of your lovely final splash from our last ish.

1) Overlay in Upper Left-hand Corner (not a caption box, please!):

               Los Angeles, California
               9:17 pm

2) Tailless: Okay, if you could be any hero working today...who'd it be?

Page One, Panel Two

      Cut inside of a teenager's bedroom for this largest panel of the page, at least a half-SPLASH. We're looking at two Hispanic teenagers, a well-dressed, athletic 16-year-old kid named VICTOR MANCHA (who will become a new member of our cast, so design him with care!), and his overweight, more "thuggish" 16-year-old buddy, JORGE.

      This is Victor's room, which is cluttered with whatever cool, contemporary stuff you think kids would have, Adrian. However, it's important that we see some Marvel Heroes stuff in here, like a big poster of Captain America on the wall that says, *"DRUGS HURT AMERICA!"* Please leave some room for this exchange:

3) Victor: Easy. Spider-Man. No question.

4) Jorge: *Spider-Man?* You're off your meds, son. The correct answer is *Mr. Fantastic*...stretch yourself out to eight feet, get a fat NBA contract.

5) Jorge: Besides, Spidey ain't even a hero. He's just another banger.

6) Victor: Oh, he is *not.* The only people who think he's a criminal are Fox News and The Daily Bugle.

And the Bugle is, like, the least respected paper in New York City.

Page One, Panel Three

      Push in on chubby Jorge for this shot. Over his shoulder in the background, we can see a CRUDE HOMEMADE ELECTRONIC DEVICE, a blinking/flashing radio that Victor built out of spare video game console parts, old speakers, etc.

7) Jorge: What do *you* know about New York, Victor? You've barely been outside *Pasadena* before.

8) Jorge: Your mom won't even let you go to *band camp* without--

9) Electronic (from device): -kzzk- *All units, be advised...possible 10-39 in progress at East First and South San Pedro. -kzzk-*

PAGE TWO

Page Two, Panel One

      Pull out to a shot of both kids for this largest panel of the page. Jorge turns around to touch Victor's homemade radio, but Victor LEAPS UP to pull his pal away.

1) Jorge: Yo, E.T., your home planet's on the line.

2) Victor: It's not a phone, dummy, that's the *police scanner* I built. Did they just say *10-39?*

3) Jorge: I guess. Why, what's that, spaz? Naked chicks on parade?

Page Two, Panel Two

      This is just a dramatic shot of Victor, as he calmly says:

4) Victor: No, it's a masked felony.

5) Victor: That's cop talk for *super-villains.*

Page Two, Panel Three

Pull out to another shot of both teens. Jorge looks excited as hell, but Victor seems sad.

6) Jorge: Real bad guys? *Here?* We gotta check 'em out!

7) Victor: I...I can't. My curfew's 8:30 on school nights.

8) Jorge: This is a once-in-a-lifetime opportunity, Vic! We *never* get costumes out here!

9) Jorge (small, an aside): Except maybe Wonder Man, and he don't count.

Page Two, Panel Four

Push in closer on the two. Jorge looks disappointed in his crestfallen friend.

10) Victor: Sorry, Jorge. It's my mom's house, her rules.
11) Victor: What am I supposed to do? *Run away?*

12) Jorge: Fft, you're gonna look back on this and *hate* yourself someday, bro. It's like the song goes, when you're an old man, you don't regret the stuff you did...

Page Two, Panel Five

This is just a small, silent shot of Victor, longingly staring out his bedroom window.

13) Jorge (from off): ...you regret the stuff you *didn't*.

PAGE THREE

Page Three, Panel One

Cut to elsewhere in Los Angeles for this page-wide establishing shot of a classy bank on an empty, palm-lined street. There should clearly be a huge HOLE in the wall of this bank, with smoke coming out of it.

1) Overlay in Upper Left-hand Corner:

Third Bank of California
9:19 pm

Page Three, Panel Two

Cut inside the bank for this close-up of a new villain named EXCAVATOR, the 17-year-old son of Piledriver. His costume can look a bit like his father's (though maybe a different color), and we should be able to see his blonde hair sticking straight out of the top of his mask. Excavator (who has a silver SHOVEL resting on his shoulder here) is smiling at a big wad of CASH that he's holding up in front of his eyes.

2) Excavator: Scrilla fo' rilla!

3) Excavator: This haul gonna be *taut.*

Page Three, Panel Three

Pull out to the largest panel of the page (at least a half-SPLASH), as we reveal that we're just outside of a smashed-into BANK VAULT. Walking out of this vault are all four members of THE WRECKING CREW (C.B. and Mac can get you reference). THUNDERBALL, PILE-DRIVER, BULLDOZER, and WRECKER (lined up in that order) are all carrying bags of cash here. We can see Excavator in the background, taking up the rear.

4) Thunderball: Piledriver, if "Excavator" here continues affecting that manner of speech, I'm going to smash him in the face with his own enchanted *shovel.*

5) Piledriver: Settle down, Thunderball. That's just the way teenagers talk these days.

6) Bulldozer: I dunno, P.D. I still think dragging your *kid* along for this score was a dumb play. This ain't the Wrecking Crew and *Son.*

7) Wrecker: Yeah, bad enough I hadda split my power with *you* ungrateful lunks, now I gotta share it with one of your long-lost *brats?*

PAGE FOUR

Page Four, Panel One

Push in for this shot of just Piledriver, as he defends his bastard son.

1) Piledriver: Wrecker, you're the one who's always saying we gotta start thinking about the *future*, right? Well, I'm just training a new generation who can *kick up* to us when we retire.

2) Piledriver: Besides, this ain't *NYC.* It's not like there's gonna be any annoying "heroes" around to interfere with the kid's first heist.

3) Piledriver (small, an aside): Except maybe Wonder Man, and he don't count.

Page Four, Panel Two
Change angles for this largest panel of the page, a shot of Bulldozer and the curious young Excavator (and anyone else you have room to draw), as they step out of the hole in the bank wall and onto the streets of Los Angeles.

4) Excavator: Hey, 'Dozer, if this town's so ripe for the picking, how come you guys didn't jump coasts sooner?

5) Bulldozer: 'Cause L.A. used to be run by a dozen stone-cold psychos called *The Pride*.

6) Bulldozer: This was *their* turf. Any mask who tried to make a play for a slice would get sent back to the Big Apple...piece by piece.

Page Four, Panel Three
Change angles again, as Excavator turns to talk with the grumpy, crowbar-wielding Wrecker.

7) Excavator: They in stir now, Mr. Wrecker?

8) Wrecker: No, they're not "in stir," you annoying piece of...

9) Wrecker: The Pride is *dead*, okay? They were betrayed by their spoiled children, in what should have been a valuable *lesson* to every hood who's got an "accident" or two out there.

Page Four, Panel Four
Change angles one last time, as Piledriver lovingly puts his arm around his son.

10) Piledriver: You got nothing to worry about with *my* boy, Wrecks. He's a chip off the old.

11) Someone's Voice (from off): Hey, Village People!

PAGE FIVE

Page Five, Panel One
Cut over to the street in front of the off-panel Wrecking Crew for this largest panel of the page, at least a half-SPLASH. It's a heroic shot of four of our Runaways: GERT, NICO, KAROLINA and MOLLY (lined up in that order, please). I'm sure we'll talk about our characters' new looks before we begin, but these girls should look confident and tough as hell here, Adrian! They don't have costumes, weapons, or even their dinosaur, but they still look ready to kick @$#.

1) Gert: Step away from the minor.

2) Molly: Or else you're in for some *major*...

3) Molly (small, an aside): ...you know, bad stuff.

Page Five, Panel Two
Cut back to the Wrecking Crew, who are all staring at the off-panel Runaways. They look super-confused, except for the hard-headed Bulldozer, who's just smiling here.

4) Thunderball: The hell is this?

5) Bulldozer: I don't know, but I'll take a box of *Thin Mints*.

Page Five, Panel Three
Cut over to Nico and Karolina.

6) Nico: Listen, we don't care about whatever money you stole. We know the bank is insured.

7) Nico: Just give us the *kid*, and you can be on your way.

8) Karolina: Haven't you seen the news, Ricky? Your grandparents are worried *sick* about you.

PAGE SIX

Page Six, Panel One
Cut over to Piledriver and his son. Excavator is defiant, but his old man is looking back at his off-panel crewmates like a proud papa.

1) Excavator: My *grandparents*? Those stank old fogies can choke on their *dentures* for all I care. I'm running with my *dad* now.

2) Piledriver: Check it out, four ladies fighting over him already.

3) Piledriver: Told you he takes after his pops.

Page Six, Panel Two
Cut back to a pissed-off Nico and Karolina, as Karolina RIPS off her own bracelet. She begins to GLOW with her alien power.

4) Nico: And that concludes the *negotiation* segment of our program.

5) Nico: Karolina?

6) <u>Karolina</u>: Plan B it is, boss.

Page Six, Panel Three
  Pull out to the largest panel of the page for a big group shot of all of our players, as a now-floating Karolina BLASTS Piledriver, knocking him backwards!

7) <u>SFX</u>: *KASCHOWW*

8) <u>Excavator</u>: DAD!

Page Six, Panel Four
  This is just a shot of the crowbar-wielding Wrecker, as he yells out an order.

9) <u>Wrecker</u>: They're *muties!*

10) <u>Wrecker</u>: Light 'em up!

PAGE SEVEN

Page Seven, Panel One
  Cut over to Karolina (still floating and firing at the off-panel Wrecking Crew) and Molly, who's beneath her, angrily punching one of her own hands in preparation for battle.

1) <u>Karolina</u>: Excuse me.

2) <u>Karolina</u>: I'm an *extraterrestrial*...and proud *of* it, thank you very much.

3) <u>Molly</u>: Besides, the word "mutie" is really offensive to people like me, you freakin' *racists.*

Page Seven, Panel Two
  Cut over to Excavator, who's running right at us. He has his enchanted shovel raised over his head.

4) <u>Excavator</u>: I'll *kill* you!

5) <u>Excavator</u>: I'll kill--

Page Seven, Panel Three
  Pull out to the largest panel of the page, as Excavator SWINGS the shovel into Molly's head. Molly doesn't even flinch as the magic tool SNAPS IN HALF across her little skull.

6) <u>SFX</u>: *KRACK*

Page Seven, Panel Four
  This is just a small close-up of the frowning Molly, her eyes GLOWING brightly here.

7) <u>Molly</u>: Too bad.

8) <u>Molly</u>: Our club coulda used another boy.

Page Seven, Panel Five
  Pull out to a bigger shot, as Molly PUNCHES Excavator in the gut, sending him FLYING down the street!

  No Copy *((KAAPOW!!))*

PAGE EIGHT

Page Eight, Panel One
  We're with Nico in the foreground of this shot, as she yells at the off-panel Molly. Behind him, Wrecker is approaching, with his crowbar at the ready.

1) <u>Nico</u>: Molly, go sit on him or something!

2) <u>Nico</u>: We'll finish off the grown-ups!

3) <u>Wrecker</u>: Sister, you just earned yourself a taste of the *big stick.*

Page Eight, Panel Two
  This is just a shot of Nico, as she turns to shoot us a scary look. Her hair is beginning to blow with mystical force.

4) <u>Nico</u>: Bet mine's bigger than yours.

Page Eight, Panel Three
  Pull out for another shot of Wrecker and Nico. A stunned Wrecker DROPS his crowbar as the GLOWING STAFF OF ONE begins *growing* out of a pained Nico's chest!

5) <u>Wrecker</u>: Ah, crap.

6) <u>Wrecker</u>: Not *witches.* I *hate*--

Page Eight, Panel Four
  Pull out to the largest panel of the page, as Nico aims her fully-formed, glowing staff at Wrecker, who instantaneously BREAKS into a hundred different pieces! Adrian, this shouldn't be the least bit gory, it's more like a *picture* of Wrecker being torn into many little pieces. No blood or guts!

7) <u>Nico (creepy font)</u>: DECONSTRUCT.

8) <u>Wrecker</u>: *NOOOOO!*

PAGE NINE

Page Nine, Panel One
        Change angles, as a flying Karolina SWOOPS down next to the staff-wielding Nico, who's standing next to all of the pieces of Wrecker. Karolina looks concerned.

1) <u>Karolina</u>: Nico!

2) <u>Nico</u>: It's all right, Karolina. He'll come together in an hour or two...probably.

3) <u>Karolina</u>: But I thought you could only use the Staff of One after your *blood* was shed? And you never...

Page Nine, Panel Two
        This is just a small silent shot of Nico, as she looks over at the off-panel Karolina, and shoots her a knowing look.

        No Copy

Page Nine, Panel Three
        And this is just a small shot of the glowing Karolina, as she finally understands what's going on.

4) <u>Karolina (small, under her breath)</u>: Oh. Right.

5) <u>Karolina (small, under her breath)</u>: That time of the month...

6) <u>Another Voice (from off)</u>: ENOUGH!

Page Nine, Panel Four
        Cut over to Thunderball and Gert for this largest panel of the page. Thunderball is menacingly SWINGING his wrecking ball in a circle over his head, as he approaches a confident Gert, who's backing towards a nearby tree.

7) <u>Thunderball</u>: You girls stand down *posthaste*...or I smash your friend here into oblivion.

PAGE TEN

Page Ten, Panel One
        Push in closer on Gert and Thunderball. Thunderball suddenly looks a little concerned.

1) <u>Gert</u>: Bad idea, Mean Green.

2) <u>Gert</u>: I've got the power to make grown men lose control of their *bowels.*

3) <u>Thunderball</u>: Really...?

Page Ten, Panel Two
        Cut back to Gert for this largest panel of the page, as OLD LACE suddenly comes LEAPING out from behind the nearby tree. The velociraptor's mouth is wide open here, so she can show off her fangs.

4) <u>Gert</u>: More or less.

5) <u>SFX by Old Lace (not in a balloon, please!)</u>: *RAAAARRR*

Page Ten, Panel Three
        Change angles on the three. As Old Lace POUNCES on top of a fallen Thunderball, Gert just shakes her head.

6) <u>Thunderball</u>: AHHHHHH!

7) <u>Gert</u>: Why couldn't my 'rents have given you to me for my *bat mitzvah*, Old Lace? A telepathic velociraptor from the 87th Century would have made middle school a lot more tolerab--

Page Ten, Panel Four
        Push in close on Gert, as a FIST (belonging to Bulldozer) suddenly enters the frame and PUNCHES Gert in the face, knocking her glasses off!

8) <u>SFX</u>: *THWACK*

PAGE ELEVEN

Page Eleven, Panel One
        Change angles to reveal that BULLDOZER is now standing over Gert, who's fallen on her butt. She's reaching for her glasses here. Bulldozer is standing in the middle of the street, and we can't see anyone except for him and Gert in this shot.

1) <u>Bulldozer</u>: I got you all figured out, fatty.

2) <u>Bulldozer</u>: Wizards, gene freaks, *time travelers*... you're *The Pride's* kids, ain't you?

3) <u>Gert</u>: Wow, maybe your head isn't as dense as it *looks*...which is too bad, considering what's about to land on *top* of it.

Page Eleven, Panel Two

Push in for this tight shot of Bulldozer, who nervously looks up, as a DARK SHADOW suddenly falls over him.

4) Bulldozer: Huh?

Page Eleven, Panel Three

Pull out to the largest panel of the page, a three-quarter SPLASH, as the Runaways' LEAPFROG suddenly comes SMASHING down in the middle of the street, presumably squashing Bulldozer flat! The ship narrowly misses Gert, who protects her face with her arm as the ship loudly LANDS inches away from her.

5) SFX:
K
R
O
O
O
M

PAGE TWELVE

Page Twelve, Panel One

Cut into the control panels of the Leapfrog, as CHASE looks out at us! He's wearing racing gloves, and maybe some kind of new goggles resting on his forehead. We can talk about his new look, Adrian, whatever you like...

1) Chase: Sorry I'm late, baby!

2) Chase: I totally forgot to gas up the Leapfrog last night. Had to "borrow" ninety gallons of unleaded from the Circle A...

Page Twelve, Panel Two

Cut back down to the street for this shot of an excited Molly, who's now standing next to Gert (who's putting her glasses back on).

3) Gert (small, an aside): We are the worst good guys of all time.

4) Molly: Chase!

5) Molly: Did you see who we got to beat up tonight? Their costumes were really pretty!

Page Twelve, Panel Three

Pull out to the largest panel of the page

for this group shot. Chase is now walking down out of the opening mouth/ramp of the Leapfrog, as he approaches the assembled girls. A still-glowing Karolina looks pissed, but Gert (standing next to Old Lace) tries to calm her down. Nico is looking off in the direction of the off-panel Excavator. We can see POLICE CARS approaching in the distant background.

6) Chase: What did we talk about, Mol? Costumes are *gay*.

7) Karolina: Hey! I warned you, misuse that word one more time and--

8) Gert: Save it, Karolina. If we're not legs up in the next thirty seconds, the pigs are gonna send us back to *foster care*.

9) Nico: What about the boy, Gert? Are we really just going to let him get hauled off to *juvie?* I mean, he's in the same boat as us.

Page Twelve, Panel Four

This is just a small shot of Gert.

10) Gert: No, I'd say he went overboard the second he saw his father as someone to *look up* to.

11) Gert: Let him go, Nico. No offense to your drearily departed boyfriend, but the last thing we need is another *Alex* to stab us in the back.

Page Twelve, Panel Five

And this is just a silent shot of a somber Nico, still looking in the direction of the off-panel Excavator.

12) Gert (from off): Face it, some kids are a *lost cause...*

PAGE THIRTEEN

Page Thirteen, Panel One

Cut to later that night for this establishing shot of a little church in Los Angeles. In the foreground of this shot, we should *clearly* see one of those CHURCH SIGNS with movable letters that reads:

1) Sign in Foreground:
Excelsior Meeting - 9:30
Church Basement

Page Thirteen, Panel Two

Cut into a dimly lit church basement for

this largest panel of the page, a nice semi-SPLASH. We're behind a row of four people sitting in folding chairs, but we can't see their faces yet. We *can* see the two young people standing in front of them: MICKEY MUSASHI (the New Warrior's Turbo) and PHIL URICH (the former heroic Green Goblin). Mickey and Phil are both wearing cool, contemporary clothing. They're both about 22-years-old, so they should look older than our Runaways, but younger than regular Marvel heroes like Captain America. Phil is giving a little wave to everybody, as Mickey introduces herself. Please leave some room for their brief opening remarks:

2) <u>Mickey</u>: Right, so...as some of you already know, my name is Michiko Musashi, but pretty much everybody calls me *Mickey.*

3) <u>Mickey</u>: I moved here three months ago after I got a job with the Los Angeles Times, thanks to a recommendation from my good pal, Phil Urich.

4) <u>Phil</u>: Howdy. Mickey and I have been talking about starting a group like this for a while now, so we really appreciate you guys coming out to our first meeting.

5) <u>Phil</u>: We don't exactly have a budget or anything, so we're starting off small, but we hope to expand Excelsior into a *nationwide* outreach program someday soon.

Page Thirteen, Panel Three
This is just a close-up of Mickey, as she makes this dramatic revelation:

6) <u>Mickey</u>: Like everyone here tonight, Phil and I are former teenage superheroes.

PAGE FOURTEEN

Page Fourteen, Panel One
Change angles on Mickey, as she reveals her secret origin. Remember, this whole scene should be dark and shadowy, Adrian, eerily lit from above!

1) <u>Mickey</u>: From the time I was a sophomore in college up until a few months ago, I'd been living a double life as the New Warrior's *Turbo.*

2) <u>Mickey</u>: But late last year, I was fighting some Z-lister, and I had this...this *epiphany.* I realized that I could do more good with my *education* than I ever could with some hi-tech *costume.* That's when I decided to get back into investigative journalism.

Page Fourteen, Panel Two
Change angles for this largest panel of the page, a shot of Mickey, as she turns her attention to one of the people seated in the first row (we can't see the others yet). This is CHRIS POWELL, the 19-year-old alter ego of Darkhawk (again, our esteemed editors will get you reference, Adrian!).

3) <u>Mickey</u>: Anyway, I'm obviously not the only one here with a story like that. Chris, why don't you keep it going?

4) <u>Chris</u>: Oh, uh, sure. My name's Chris Powell, and I'm...well, I *used* to be Darkhawk.

5) <u>Chris</u>: I found this *amulet* back when I was in high school, and it changed me into this...this *thing.* You know the drill.

Page Fourteen, Panel Three
This is just a shot of Chris, as he hangs his head and nervously recounts how he got here.

6) <u>Chris</u>: I used the powers it gave me as a *vigilante* for a couple of years, which was cool and all, but I...

7) <u>Chris</u>: I started having these *nightmares.* Really intense ones. I mean, I was in New York when some pretty bad stuff went down, and I...I just had to get away.

Page Fourteen, Panel Four
Change angles, as Phil Urich walks over and puts a hand on Chris' shoulder. Phil looks over at another one of the off-panel guests at this meeting.

8) <u>Chris</u>: I'm not cut out for seeing all the stuff I've seen, you know? I don't think *anyone* my age is. I'm sure I sound like a *coward,* but--

9) <u>Phil</u>: You're a brave guy, Chris. You always have been.

10) <u>Phil</u>: Julie, why don't you take the floor?

PAGE FIFTEEN

Page Fifteen, Panel One
Cut over to another guest for this largest panel of the page, as a smiling JULIE POWER stands, like a teacher's pet addressing her speech class. Julie is the grown-up version of Lightspeed from *Power Pack.* She's about 18 years old here, so she should look older than the Runaways' girls, but younger than

Mickey. She's wearing something sexy, but not too slutty. She looks like she could be a movie star.

1) Julie: *Ahem*. Thank you, Mr. Urich. Hi, everybody. I'm Julie Power. And yes, before you ask, that *is* my real name.

2) Julie: Actually, I've had *lots* of names over the years: Lightspeed, Starstreak, Molecula, Mistress of Density...

Page Fifteen, Panel Two
Push in closer on Julie, as she suddenly gets more serious.

3) Julie: See, when I was just ten years old, my brothers and sister and I met someone from...well, from far away. Long story short, we became *Power Pack*.

4) Julie: When my siblings and I were fighting crime, I thought it was all just fun and games. I had no idea I was actually being robbed of a *normal childhood*.

Page Fifteen, Panel Three
Pull out for this shot of Julie and Mickey, as Mickey politely interrupts her.

5) Julie: With the help of a lot of therapy, I'm trying to get some of that innocence *back*.

6) Julie: I've always loved fantasy and drama, so I'm living in Hollywood now, just taking auditions and looking for an agent. So, ah, if anyone wants to *network* after this...

7) Mickey: Thanks, Julie. You want to share, Johnny?

Page Fifteen, Panel Four
Cut over to JOHNNY GALLO, the 19-year-old kid who used to be the Slingers' Ricochet. He looks like $%@# here, disheveled and depressed.

8) Johnny: I don't know, man. I...I feel totally outclassed here. I mean, you guys have probably never even *heard* of me.

9) Johnny: My team...my team didn't even have a *name*. We were just a bunch of Spider-Man wannabes. I used to be this guy called *Ricochet*.

Page Fifteen, Panel Five
Change angles on poor ol' Johnny, as he continues talking:

10) Johnny: When my powers first materialized, I thought fulltime hero-ing was gonna be my *life*. And for a while, I guess it was. It was *awesome*.

11) Johnny: But before I knew it, it was *over*. I'd even *look* for crimes and stuff, but by the time I'd get to one, somebody like *Iron Fist* or *Moon Knight* was already taking care of it.

12) Johnny: I wasn't a superhero...I was *superfluous*.

PAGE SIXTEEN

Page Sixteen, Panel One
Pull out to a larger panel, as Mickey and Phil try to console Johnny.

1) Johnny: And I really loved the spotlight, man. What kid wouldn't? But when you get so much, so young, so *fast*...nobody tells you how to deal when that spotlight inevitably shuts off, you know?

2) Mickey: Well, we founded Excelsior to help with *every* stage of your transition into adulthood and a healthy civilian life. Right, Phil?

3) Phil: Absolutely. I'd be lying if I said I didn't enjoy *my* time as the Green Goblin, but now I know what a dangerous message people like us were sending to impressionable young--

Page Sixteen, Panel Two
Cut over to CHAMBER, our last member of Excelsior, as he suddenly JUMPS to his feet and OPENS his bandages, exposing the GLOWING BIOKINETIC FIRE in his chest.

4) Chamber (unique font): Hold the bleedin' phone!

5) Chamber (unique font): This kid's the *Green Goblin*?

Page Sixteen, Panel Three
Pull out to the largest panel of the page for a big group shot, as Phil nervously backs away from the glowing Chamber. All of the other kids look scared as Mickey tries to calm down Chamber.

6) Phil: Oh, I...I wasn't the *evil* Green Goblin. I just found one of his suits, and used the equipment to protect--

7) Chamber (unique font): There was a *good* Green Goblin? That is the absolute *stupidest* thing I've ever heard!

8) Mickey: Jonothan, why don't you put your *blast furnace* away and introduce yourself to the nice--

Page Sixteen, Panel Four

This is just a shot of Chamber, as he begins resealing himself with the black wraps that hide the big glowing hole in his face and chest.

9) Chamber (unique font): The name's *Jono,* luv. Or Chamber. Whichever strikes.

10) Chamber (unique font): Right then, Reader's Digest: I'm a mutant, did some time as a soldier with the X-Men after I blew half me own face off. A group of sods called Weapon X patched me up, but I went and ripped a *new* hole in myself when some drunk in Fresno made me mad.

11) Chamber (unique font): Anyway, just enduring this sob-fest for the free pizza I read about in the email.

PAGE SEVENTEEN

Page Seventeen, Panel One

Change angles for this shot of Julie, Johnny and Mickey. Julie and Johnny are staring at the off-panel Chamber, while Mickey pulls out her little CELL PHONE.

1) Julie: Pizza? I hope this isn't insensitive, Jono, but if you don't have a *mouth...?*

2) Johnny: Wait, you were part of the *X-Men?* As in, Professor *Xavier's* X-Men? They wouldn't even return my--

3) SFX (from off): *DEET DEET DOO*

4) Mickey: If you guys could excuse me for a second, that's probably my *editor.*

Page Seventeen, Panel Two

Pull out to the largest panel of the page, as Mickey walks towards us, away from the talkative group in the background of this shot, and into the shadowy back of the church basement. She's talking on her phone now.

5) Mickey: Musashi here.

6) Tailless (electronic): Way to go, girl. Your little group's a cool idea, very well executed.

Page Seventeen, Panel Three

Push in close on Mickey, who suddenly looks angry and a little sacred.

7) Mickey: Who *is* this? How'd you get this number?

8) Tailless (electronic): Yeah, that's not really important right now, Mick.

9) Tailless (electronic): What is important is that there are other people out there who need Excelsior's help. Not *former* heroes, but underage kids who are putting their necks on the line even as we--

Page Seventeen, Panel Four

Cut to an unknown location for this shot of A SHADOWY FIGURE. This is a male, but we can't tell who it is, or where he's at, Adrian!

10) Tailless (electronic): I didn't start wearing a mask *yesterday,* pal. If you think I'm gonna start running *errands* for some mystery benefactor, you can kiss my--

11) From Figure: All I'm asking your team to do is help me find five runaways...

12) From Figure: ...and in exchange, I'll give your organization *one million dollars,* enough to reach out to every cape and cowl who's ever lived the life.

Page Seventeen, Panel Five

Finally, cut back to a quietly intrigued Mickey for this closing extreme close-up.

13) Mickey: Keep talking.

PAGE EIGHTEEN

Page Eighteen, Panel One

Cut to later that night for this establishing shot of THE LA BREA TAR PITS (if you draw those elephants in the tar, they should clearly be FAKE).

1) Overlay in Upper Left-hand Corner:

The La Brea Tar Pits
10:01 pm *((Don't put time here)).*

Page Eighteen, Panel Two

Cut into the massive caves underneath the tar pits for a three-quarter SPLASH, our first look at THE HOSTEL II! The Leapfrog is parked here, and the kids are walking away from it, in this order from left to right: Molly, Karolina (no longer glowing), Gert (with Old Lace), Chase, Karolina, and Nico (no longer holding her staff). The kids can just be smallish figures in this torch-lit shot. They're walking underneath a GIANT FRAMED PORTRAIT of the twelve members of THE PRIDE, all in their villain costumes. Feel free to fill the lair with whatever other cool super-villain crap you wanna draw, Adrian!

2) <u>Molly</u>: I wish we had put our hideout under an *In & Out Burger*. I'm so sick of eating whatever junk my mom *pickled* down here before she...you know.

3) <u>Karolina</u>: Just be glad we have *someplace* for our new Hostel, Molly.

4) <u>Gert</u>: Yeah, if we hadn't found our parents' old *lair*, the five of us would still be cloaked on Venice Beach, sleeping in the same smelly ship.

5) <u>Chase</u>: With all these evil fruit loops to beat down, we're practically living inside the 'Frog, *anyway*. That Space Ghost-looking *Flag-Smasher* guy last week, *Typeface* the week before that...

6) <u>Nico</u>: Well, this is *our* fault, you know. We're the ones who created the power vacuum.

PAGE NINETEEN

Page Nineteen, Panel One
Push in on Chase and Gert. As Chase makes a joke, Gert blushes and elbows him in the side playfully. In the background, we can see a disgusted Molly rolling her eyes.

1) <u>Chase</u>: Heh, "power vacuum." That should be Gert's new codename.

2) <u>Gert</u>: You're disgusting.

3) <u>Molly</u>: Can you two go back to hating each other, please? It made me barf in my mouth less.

Page Nineteen, Panel Two
Cut over to Nico, looking deadly severe.

4) <u>Nico</u>: I'm *serious*. Us taking down The Pride was like the U.S. taking down *Saddam*. We got rid of a monster, but we didn't plan for what would happen *next*.

5) <u>Nico</u>: Our parents may have been awful people, but at least they maintained some kind of...of *order*.

Page Nineteen, Panel Three
Change angles for this shot of Chase, Karolina and Nico. Chase is pointing at Gert's parents' TIME MACHINE, the gazebo-looking thing you drew during our first season, which is sitting dusty and broken in a corner of this crowded old lair. Karolina and Nico are berating Chase.

6) <u>Chase</u>: Hey, if you want your mommy and daddy back so bad, why don't you hop in the Yorkes' old *time machine* and rescue 'em from the past?

7) <u>Karolina</u>: Because she *doesn't* want them back, Chase. She's just saying we have a responsibility to clean up their *mess*, right, Nico?

8) <u>Nico</u>: And for the son of two mad *scientists*, you sure do have trouble comprehending the fact that Gert's parents' 4D-thing has been *busted* for--

Page Nineteen, Panel Four
Pull out to the largest panel of the page for a big group shot. The kids all cover their eyes, as ANOTHER version of the Yorkes' time machine appears in the lair in a blinding flash of light! We can see a figure silhouetted inside this time machine, but we can't see who it is yet.

9) <u>SFX</u>: *FWASH*

PAGE TWENTY

Page Twenty, Panel One
Cut over to this newly arrived time machine for a three-quarter SPLASH. Standing in the middle of this steamy contraption is a SUPER-HEROINE. She's about 35 years old, five-foot-six, raven-haired, busty, thin, and very, very attractive. She's wearing a long cape, skirt, boots, and a tight corset-type top (her costume is torn and dirty in places, like she's just survived a terrible fight). As she steps into the low-hanging fog surrounding the bottom of this machine, she's clutching her stomach, which appears to be bleeding (though we need to be very subtle with this...maybe it blends in with her dark-colored outfit?).

1) <u>Heroine</u>: Please...please tell me what year this is...

Page Twenty, Panel Two
We're looking over the Heroine's shoulder in the foreground of this shot, over at an angry Gert and a confused Old Lace in the background.

2) Heroine: Oh...Karolina's still here...

3) Heroine: Must be *2005*...

4) Gert: Lady, you take another step, and my dinosaur will *end* you.

Page Twenty, Panel Three
This is just an extreme close-up of the Heroine, as she drops this bombshell:

5) Heroine: I seriously doubt that, Gertrude.

6) Heroine: Seeing how I'm *you*...

PAGE TWENTY-ONE

Page Twenty-one, Panel One
Pull out to the largest panel of the page for a big group shot, as the Heroine (still clutching her stomach) limps towards the stunned kids. The Heroine kindly strokes a friendly Old Lace's head, as the dino brushes up against her.

1) Nico: *What?*

2) Gert: She's *lying.* I wouldn't be caught *dead* in that get-up.

3) Heroine: Funny choice of words, kid...and you'll realize how much things can *change*...in about twenty years...when you start leading the *Avengers*...

Page Twenty-one, Panel Two
Change angles for this shot of Heroine and a wide-eyed Molly.

4) Molly: Gert's gonna be a *super hero?*

5) Heroine: It's not as fun as it sounds, Mol...

6) Heroine: She's going to be betrayed...by someone she's *stupid* enough to put on her team...

Page Twenty-one, Panel Three
Change angles for this shot of Heroine and Chase, as Chase rushes over to help hold up the injured woman.

7) Heroine: I barely escaped...with my life. He just *slaughtered* my Avengers...used my *files* to kill the others...

8) Heroine: Hisako and her X-Men, Daredevil, the

Fantastic Fourteen...he murdered *all* of them...every hero on the planet...

9) Chase: *Who* did?

Page Twenty-one, Panel Four
This is just a close-up of Heroine, as she looks at the off-panel Chase and says:

10) Heroine: A supposed "champion" named *Victorious.* He's the most powerful man...on the *planet*...

11) Heroine: Please...you're the future's only *hope*... Iron Woman sacrificed her *life* to help power my one last trip...because I need you children...to *stop* him...

PAGE TWENTY-TWO

Page Twenty-two, Panel One
Change angles for this shot of Karolina and the Heroine, who's still being held up by Chase. Heroine is reaching for something in her belt here.

1) Karolina: Us?

2) Karolina: Ma'am, how are we supposed to stop something if the *grown-up* us's can't?

3) Heroine: You have to find Victorious when he was just a boy...before he becomes too strong...

Page Twenty-two, Panel Two
Push in on Heroine, as she holds up a torn-at-the-edges, slightly faded photo of VICTOR MANCHA, who looks exactly like he did at the beginning of this issue!

4) Heroine: His real name is *Victor Mancha.*

5) Heroine: He grew up...in Pasadena...

Page Twenty-two, Panel Three
Pull out to a shot of Chase and the Heroine, as she begins to slump to the floor. Chase kneels with her, gently easing her to the ground in his arms.

6) Heroine: Don't trust him. He's not who he says he is...I knew only you guys would understand...

7) Heroine: His father...is a villain from your time...the greatest evil...in the *universe*...

8) <u>Chase</u>: What's that mean? Who's this guy the son of?

Page Twenty-two, Panel Four
Push in closer on the two. Chase is cradling Older Gert much like Younger Gert cradled him when he "died" back in Issue #15. The Heroine lovingly looks up at Chase through half-shut eyes and breathes her last breath here.

9) <u>Heroine (small, groggy)</u>: Sweet Chase...

10) <u>Heroine (small, trailing off)</u>: In all those years... I never told you...how much I loved...*

PAGE TWENTY-THREE

Page Twenty-three, Panel One
Pull out to a larger shot of Chase and the now-lifeless Heroine. He's still looking down at her.

No Copy

Page Twenty-three, Panel Two
Cut over to the other Runaways (and Old Lace). Karolina covers her mouth in horror. The others don't know what to say.

1) <u>Chase (from off)</u>: She's dead.

Page Twenty-three, Panel Three
Pull out to the largest panel of the page, as the girls begin to argue.

2) <u>Molly</u>: I'm...I'm really sorry, Gert.

3) <u>Gert</u>: That was *not* me! This is probably just another...another *lie* from our parents, one last *mind-freak* from the grave!

4) <u>Karolina</u>: But Old Lace seemed pretty sure--

Page Twenty-three, Panel Four
Cut over to Nico, as she tries to take control of the situation.

5) <u>Nico</u>: *Quiet.* Let's think about this for a second.

6) <u>Nico</u>: What if this woman *was* telling the truth? Even if there really *is* someone out there who's gonna kill every hero on earth someday, what do we do about it *now*?

PAGE TWENTY-FOUR

Page Twenty-four, SPLASH
Finally, we close on this dramatic SPLASH (with room at the *bottom* of this page for title and closing credits, please!). This is a somewhat high-angle downshot on Chase, still cradling the Heroine's lifeless body (she still has Victor's photo in her hands). We can now see that Chase has TEARS streaming down his face, as he looks up at us, and through angrily gritted teeth, says:

1) <u>Chase</u>: We find him...and we rip his damn heart out.

2) <u>Title</u>:   **TRUE BELIEVERS**
                chapter one